THEY CALL IT
WRESTLING

A PICTORIAL ANTHOLOGY OF
THE AMERICAN WRESTLER

THEY CALL IT
WRESTLING

A PICTORIAL ANTHOLOGY OF
THE AMERICAN WRESTLER

WADE SCHALLES

LEISURE PRESS

A publication of
Leisure Press
597 Fifth Avenue, New York, N.Y. 10017

Library of Congress Catalog Card Number: 82-81800

ISBN: 88011-074-0

Jacket design: Brian Groppe
Front Jacket Illustration: Ted Watts
Book design: Nasrine Greene

NEW YORK

National Champion Cowboys

**All of these Oklahoma State
athletes during this 1930 season
finished as either National
Champion or runner-up.**

Dedication

In life, the greater the goal the tougher the fight. Athletes who achieve understand this and accept the challenge. Ray Murphy is one such dedicated fighter. This book is dedicated to him and to his challenge.

This 1929 bout drew over 500 spectators.
Referees were classy individuals then,
too!

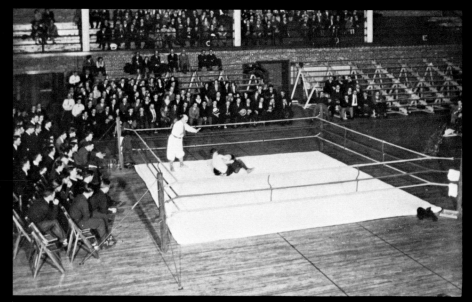

Oklahoma State Cowboys

University of Northern Iowa's Gym

A typical Ed Gallagher workout during
the early 1930's. Notice the horses that
support this 20 x 20 canvas-covered
three-roped area.

Photo Credits

Bill Smith
Dick Greene
Altar Photographic Studios
Amateur Athletic Union
Life Magazine
Toledo Blade
University of Wisconsin
Oklahoma State Redskin
Mankato State College
Brigham Young Athletics
Hal Williams
Paul Barker
Moorhead State College
Amateur Wrestling News
University of Tennessee-Chattanooga
Mike O'Neal
Mike Miller
Steve Brown
Jack Ackerman
Bob Daemmrich
Duane Hopp
Joe Kirn
Clemson Tiger
Wylie Mitchell
David L. Holman
Chris Poff
University of Iowa Audiovisual Center
Mike Chapman

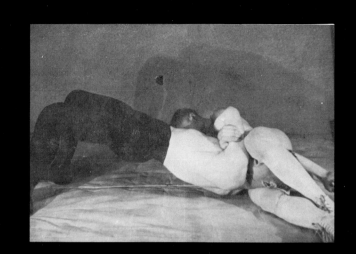

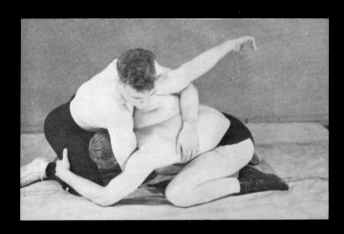

Maybe I should have stayed home with the visiting in-laws.

Contributors

Stan Able
Ben Bennett
Tommy Chesbro
Lucille Connor
Michael Connor
Bob Dillanger
Elias George
Ron Goode
Jim Grayes
Joe Henson
John Hoke
Warner Holzer
Ken Kraft
Harold Nichols
Jack Reily
Don Sayenga
Thad Turner
Pam Watson
Vince Zuaro

One of the most memorable matches in the history of NCAA wrestling—Larry Owens' stunning upset of previously undefeated Dan Gable in the 1970 Nationals.

Financial Contributors

Glen and Mary Lou Brand
Clemson University Athletic Department
Art Connorton
Chuck Coryea
Fred Davis
Bob and Rosemary Dieli
Drexel Wrestling Club
Tom Elling
Ron F. Gray
Jim Grayes
Rea Hartley
Indiana University Wrestlers
T.J. Kerr
Jim Morgan
Norm Palovcsik
Resilite Sports Products
Raymond E. Sparks

But Dad, you have to remember that it's only a wrestling match.

Introduction

As I see it, there are two reasons to write a book—for the obvious financial rewards and the personal satisfaction received by accomplishing something worthwhile. The only thing that varies from author to author is the amount of emphasis placed on one area as opposed to another. Personally, I have received enough financial rewards through wrestling for it to be erroneous on my part to use such as the main motivational force. The real reason for undertaking such a project was strictly personal; it is an attempt to repay the sport in a small way for all it has given the Schalles family.

Wrestling has to be one of the greatest sports in the history of mankind. It provides every youngster with an opportunity to accomplish something by himself in plain view of his peers. That something can only be achieved after one has made a commitment to excellence, set formidable goals, and paid the price to attain those goals. During that period one develops many fond memories of experiences shared with teammates, friendships forged through combat, and opportunities that develop because of one's dedication to the sport.

It is my hope that your enjoyment of this book is two-fold. The first and most obvious way is to enjoy each photograph for its content and the story it tells. The second, not so obvious reason is to give you the chance to say "Ah, do I remember when. . ." or "It's been ages since I did that." So enjoy yourself and escape into the past!

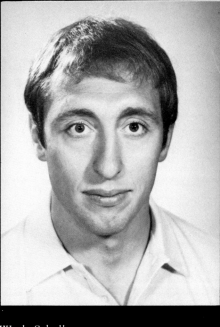

Wade Schalles

About the Author

Wade Schalles became nationally known during his years at Clarion State College and helped the Golden Eagles become one of the top wrestling schools in the country. Not content with winning four NCAA titles, Schalles moved on to the international scene and became a world champion and gold medal winner of Tbilisi International. His unique style of wrestling was years ahead of its time and helped influence today's wide-open philosophy of wrestling.

A bout-by-bout count of "Wondrous Wade's" astounding career gives him 806 wins against 49 losses with 612 pins. He presently holds the NCAA, national and world records for most wins, which is chronicled in the *Guinness Book of World Records*.

After retiring from active competition, Wade moved to South Carolina and founded the Clemson University wrestling program; within three years he steered the Tigers to a top-15 finish nationally. He presently is the head wrestling coach at Old Dominion University in Norfolk, Virginia.

On a national level, Wade served as head coach for the 1983 Pan American games in Caracus, Venezuela, and his sambo squads brought back both team titles. He currently serves on the Board of Directors of USA Wrestling, holds a seat on the National Sambo Committee, and is the national coach for sambo wrestling.

I passed up basketball to do this!

What do ya mean I can't call a time-out and discuss this with you?
Coach, I forget what to do from here!

(*Bowlsby pinning State opponent to tie the match*)

We have come a long way . . .

1960 OSU v OU

and then . . .

. . . as now we still pack them in and certainly
entertain them. . .

1972 Iowa v Iowa State

Borders takes Gizoni down early in the match. . .
Borders built up a 6-3 margin going into the third.

Gizoni began his comeback by escaping from Borders at the outset of Period Three.

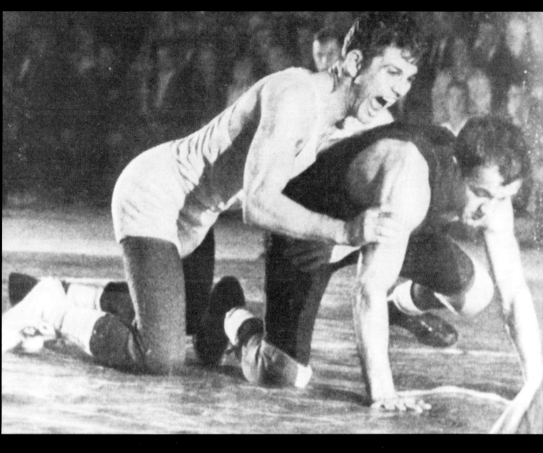

This late third period takedown enabled Gizoni to squeeze out a 7-6 victory

Stands with his first captain, William Smith, who was the 1917 Southwest Conference champion at two different weights that year.

Gallagher, Ed — Oklahoma State Coach (1929 to 1940

"The first Division III wrestler to ever challenge the big boys and win it all in 1978. Made the spinning setup for doubles and singles famous."

Mallory, Ken—Montclair State (top)

Gable, Dan—Iowa State

"The Babe Ruth of modern day wrestling. The person everyone tries to emulate and standards are set by."

Little talent, but what a heart.

Thrill of victory or . . .?

Lighten up!

Hull, Mitch—Wisconsin (top)

"Intensity and dedication personified."
    Duane Kleven
    Head Coach, University of Wisconsin

"Speedy takedowns have made Joe Gonzales the best 114.5 pound freestyle wrestler in the United States—perhaps the world."

Sports Illustrated; 1982

Gonzales, Joe—Cal State Bakersfield (standing)

Darkus, Kevin—Iowa State University (facing)

**Taking a dropstep forward in the execution of a firemen's carry.
Darkus defeated Rynder of Oklahoma and won the big 8s.**

"Probably the best Bar Arm specialist in the history of Brigham Young University Wrestling."
   Fred Davis
   Coach, Brigham Young University

Hansen, Laron—Brigham Young University (top)

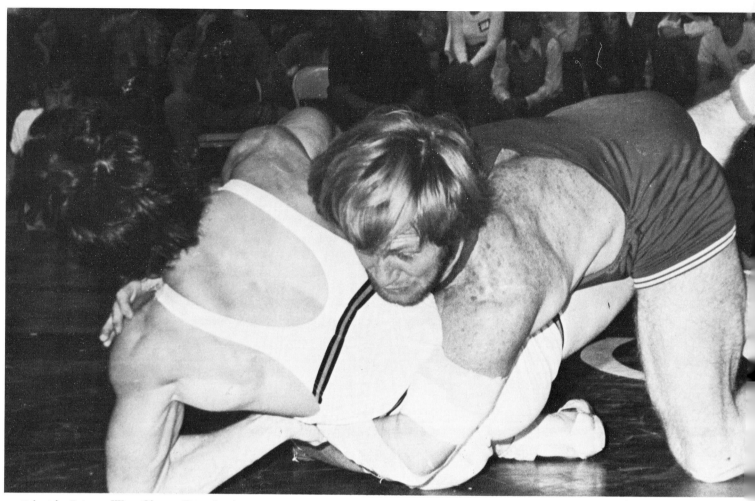

Schmidt, Brian—West Chester State (top)

"Toughest wrestler I've ever coached—undefeated in college dual competition."
Milt Collier
Head Coach, West Chester State

Mangianti, Mark—Sunkist Kids (defending)

"Real competitor in a tough weight class; determined and consistent trainer."
   Bobby Douglas
   Head Coach, Arizona State University

A solid performer who made few mental mistakes during a bout.
Note the execution of hand control.

"A quiet person who lets his ability on the mat speak for him. He
is the only individual to defeat Lee Kemp in an NCAA
tournament."

Anonymous

"Could make his opponents wrestle his style and thus dominated
them."
Dan Gable
Head Coach, University of Iowa

Yagla, Chuck—Iowa (top)

Warlick, John—Clemson University (top)

"The best lawyer in the business because he knows how to find a way to win!"
Wade Schalles
Head Coach, Clemson University

Former NCAA Champion, Ben Peterson, is momentarily in trouble against NCAA Champion-to-be Al Nacin in the 1974 Midlands.

Nancin, Al—Iowa State (top)

"A fierce competitor who loves the sport of wrestling. Because of this love, he just keeps getting better."
    Dan Gable
    Head Coach, University of Iowa

"I don't get no respect" must be the thought of Legend Ben Peterson as NCAA Champion-to-be Al Nacin has the upper half (I mean upper hand) during the 1974 Midlands.

Davis, Barry—Iowa (top)

Carr, Jimmy—Kentucky (left)

"The youngest wrestler to ever make the United States Olympic Team and just one member of the wrestling-rich Carr family."
  Anonymous

A great who peaked too soon and only made the Olympic team.

"One of the most exciting wrestlers I've ever watched because of his quickness and smoothness."
  Fletcher Carr
  Head Coach, University of Kentucky

DiGirolamo in control
of Iowa State's Johnny
Jones during the
1976 NCAAs.

"He, Rich Sanders and Wade Schalles were the first to let the big timers know that the College Division was indeed viable wrestling."

Jim Howard
Head Coach,
Oswego State

"The most complete wrestler that I have ever been associated with and a fine gentlemen."
Fred Powell
Head Coach,
Slippery Rock State

"Russ had the ability to prepare himself psychologically for competition as well as anyone I ever had compete for me."
Ken Kraft
Northwestern University Athletics

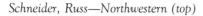

Schneider, Russ—Northwestern (top)

Steve Barrett, Oklahoma State vs. Sam Komar, Indiana

Willingham is moments away from near fall points in his struggle with Jim Mason of Michigan State.

Willingham, Randy—Oklahoma State
(top, in control)

Finals of the 1980 World Cup finds American Bobby Weaver in control and scoring points against his Russian counterpart.... Weaver and the U.S. team came away with the gold.

Weaver, Bobby—Lehigh (top)

"One of the most comfortable wrestlers in the most unorthodox positions."

"Was one of the most innovative wrestlers that I've ever seen."
Lee Allen
Olympic Greco-Roman Coach

"Possibly one of the greatest innovators in the sport to come by in a long time."
Howard Westcott
Head Coach, Portland State

Sanders, Rick—Portland State University (right)

"One of the most complete men I have worked with. Capable, thoughtful and caring. Always giving his best in whatever he does. The best wrestler I have coached."
Ed Perry
Head Coach, United States Naval Academy

Keaser, Lloyd—Navy/United States Marine Corps (left)
Mr. Ankle Pick.

"One of the finest all-round dedicated wrestlers I have had the pleasure of coaching."
Rumy Macias
Head Coach, Mankato State University

DeLeon, Al—Mankato State (right)

"Stubborn determination combined with blinding speed brought Jarrett more victories than any other Michigan wrestler."
Michigan Wrestling Office

Hubbard, Jarrett—Michigan

Haime Shinjo from the University of Washington works for the
fall against his Iowa State opponent in the 1972 Nationals.

Shinjo, Haime—Washington (top)

Brand controls Woldomar Van Cott during the 1948 Olympic
trials. Brand emerged the winner and claimed the Olympic gold
that year.

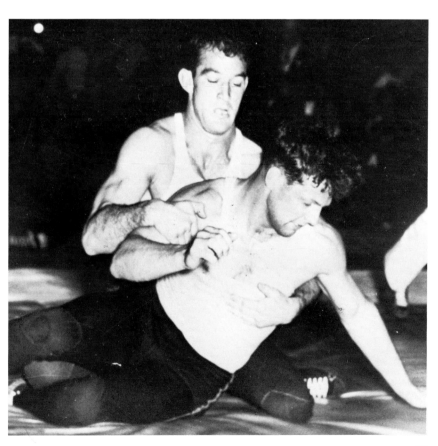

Brand, Glen—Iowa State (top)
NCAA Champion 1948

"An outstanding athlete/competitor"
Gene Davis, Olympian

Lieberman, Mike—Lehigh University

Chris Campbell tries to contain Mike Lieberman in the NCAA Finals.

Early round action at the NCAA in 1975 finds Lehigh's Mike Lieberman working for the fall.

Evans, Tommy—Oklahoma University

Evans is in for a takedown. The action took place at the 1952 Olympics held at Helsinki, Finland. Evans took the silver, losing to Olle Anderburg of Sweden in the finals.

Blass controls Penn State's Krufka during the NCAA semi-finals in 1954.

Blass, Ned—Oklahoma State University (top)
(NCAA Champion 1953-1954)

Dual meet action from 1960 finds Doug Wilson, a Big 8 finalist, controlling Paul Enochson of Colorado State.

Wilson, Doug—Oklahoma State (top)

Chis Horpel was the Babe Ruth of Stanford wrestling. Always looking for wrestling's home run, the fall.

Horpel, Chris—Stanford (throwing)

"Bill (Elbows) Simpson was a Division 1 NCAA National
  Champion and two-time all-American. A quiet leader who was
  respected by all."
     Bob Bubb
     Head Coach, Clarion State

Simpson, Bill— Clarion State College (throwing)

Mello, Dan—Portland State

"Dedicated to the sport beyond most people."
Howard Westcott
Head Coach, Portland State

"Great clinician and master of the gut wrench."

"Was a most entertaining and versatile collegiate and international wrestler."
Duane Kleven
Head Coach, University of Wisconsin

Soucie, Lourent—Wisconsin (facing top)

Kline, Gobel—Maryland (top)

On his way to another ACC crown.

**"Only wrestler to defeat Jim Nance in
college."**
    Bill Garland
    Head Coach, Moorhead State

**In this picture ...
Billberg losing to Joe James,
Oklahoma State, NCAA heavyweight
Championship final in 1964.**

Billberg, Bob— Moorhead State (right)

Kinseth, Bruce—Iowa (right)

"He has been my most prepared athlete to date."
Dan Gable
Head Coach, University of Iowa

'Jeff is one of the most self-directed and
ntelligent wrestlers today."
Doug Parker
Head Coach, Springfield College

This Brigham Young University product struggles to defeat John Needham on his way to a fourth place finish in the 1974 NCAAs.

Badger Mark Zimmer hoists Shelby Stone in the air on the way to a 12-4 victory.

Gibson, Greg—Oregon/United States Marine Corps (right)

"A man who says little but does a lot."
    Stan Dziedzic
    United States National Coach

"He makes me proud of my country."
    Eric Kopsha
    FILA Official

"One of the finest athletes in our country. It was a real pleasure to coach Greg."
    Ron Finley
    Head Coach, University of Oregon

Cavayero, Steve—SUNY Binghamton (countering duck under)

Volvia, Richard—Rutgers (right)

"He outlasted many a fine coach, being one himself with seemingly little rewards."
Jim Howard
Oswego State, Head Coach

"The history of the man indicates that he made one contribution after another to the sport of wrestling."
Joe Scalzo
Amateur Athletics Union

"The best athlete our school has ever had and one of the best wrestlers in Division III history."
Steve Erber
Head Coach, SUNY Binghamton

"Lou is an awesome competitor and one of
the finest individuals that I have had the
privilege to coach.
    Gary Taylor
    Head Coach, Rider College

DiSerafino, Lou—Rider College (top)

Tomlinson, Arlie—Oklahoma A&M (top)

Finishes up a half nelson on teammate Leroy McGuirk during a bout in 1930.

"Turner became a wrestling legend at University of Tennessee-Chattanooga in his own time. He personified pride and determination."
Jim Morgan
Head Coach, University of Tennessee-Chattanooga

Jackson, Turner—University of Tennessee-Chattanooga

"What the hell can I say—he's one of the toughest little men America has ever produced."
    Bill Weick
    United States Olympic Coach

Martin, Billy—Oklahoma State University

Heller, Charles—Clarion State, Pennsylvania (right)

"A three-time NCAA Division 1 all-American. If it weren't for a couple of wrestling giants at his weight class, he would have been a two-time National Champ."

Bob Bubb
Head Coach, Clarion State

United States Wrestling Foundation National Champion Greg Hicks is in deep against NCAA Champion Shorty Hitchcock during a 1972 bout.

Hicks, Greg—North Carolina State (right)

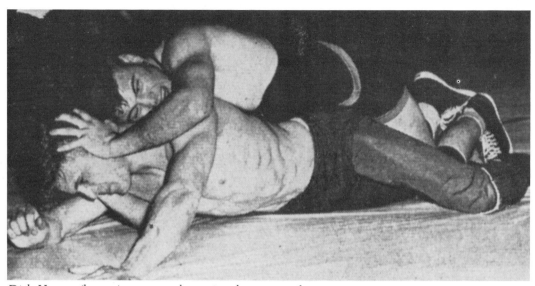

Dick Heaton (bottom)—seems to be getting the message from Nebraska's John Anderson as the two battle during season. Heaton, a junior, lost in the national semis.

"One of the most awesome heavyweights that ever took to the mats. His physical attributes were unparalleled."

Jim Howard
Head Coach, Oswego State

James, Joe—Oklahoma State

Wells, Joe—Iowa

"One ornery dude on the mat. You could tell
by his eyes."

Dan Gable
Head Coach, University of Iowa

Smith, Brad—Iowa University (control)

"It took the Iowa coaches a long time to figure what Brad needed to assure success, but when we did he became the NCAA Champ in convincing fashion."
Dan Gable
Head Coach, University of Iowa

Frick, Mike—Lehigh (control)

"Best leader both on and off the mat; he worked for everything he earned"
    Bobby Douglas
    Head Coach, Arizona State

Engineers' National Champion Mike Frick lifts his Iowa opponent, Brad Smith, during a critical bout at the NCAAs.

Severn, Dave—Arizona State University (top)

Terry, Mike—Wisconsin (left)

**Mike footsweeps Pickard of Iowa State to start
out a wild match which Terry won.**

Kinyon, Phil—Oklahoma State (lifting)

   **This bout decided who advanced to the
1961 NCAA finals at Oregon State. Phil won
this match over Fritz Fivian and the title.**

Stevens, Greg—Iowa University (control)

"Did some amazing things that the coaches
  and fans will never forget."
        Dan Gable
        Head Coach, University of Iowa

Mehnert, George (1904; 1908)

This Newark, New Jersey, native is America's only two-time Olympic Wrestling Champion.

Gray, Ron—Iowa State University

"A very smart wrestler."
Richard Volvia
Olympian

Mourlam, Keith—Iowa

"The ups and downs of what is involved in wrestling sometimes causes turmoil in one's thinking. Thankfully there have been a lot of ups in Keith's wrestling to make him better."

Dan Gable
Head Coach,
University of Iowa

Massery, Mark—Northwestern (top)

"A great competitor with the knack of knowing where he was on the mat at all times."

Kent Kraft
Northwestern University

"A great carpenter of self-character."
Dale Thomas
Head Coach, Oregon State University

Stroble, Greg—Oregon State University (top)

Maughan, Bucky—Moorhead State (top)

"Who would suspect that this little hard–nosed kid also has a great mind for the sport of wrestling."
    Jim Howard
    Head Coach, Oswego State

"I remember him, he's the guy who used to sit on his back and flip you with his feet. He was good with it too!"
    Richard Volvia
    Olympian

"A leader by example"
    Michigan Athletic Department

Churella, Mark—Michigan (in control)

Rippey, Larry—Lock Haven State (top)

"Larry could cook up the best pancakes of anyone in the wrestling world."

Jim Howard
Head Coach, Oswego State

Taylor, Chris—Iowa State (top)

Reilly, Jack—Northwestern University (1929-32) (top)

"One of the toughest, meanest, son-of-a-bitches America has ever produced.
Jim Grayes
Wrestling Promoter

"He was quite a wrist locker. If you didn't go with it, he'd break your arm."
Richard Volvia
Olympian

"He would have been a champion in any era."
Ken Kraft
a former student

"This Gentle Giant was everything his titles suggest; a great person, athlete, and friend of all."
Russ Houk
United States Olympic Team Leader

"After his death, his autopsy revealed that 400 pounds of his quarter-ton body mass was heart.

"As a wrestler, Taylor was surprisingly agile, had enormous strength and a knack for showmanship."
Sports Illustrated

"When I went for my Army physical they rejected me. I was too good-looking."
Chris Taylor on himself

Peterson, Ben—Iowa State (left)

"One of our greatest big men; a national
Champion, Olympic Champion and all-
American Young Man."

Bert Kraus
United States Wrestling Official

"A tough wrestler that could both hurt and
frustrate opponents."
   Fred Powell
   Head Coach, Slippery Rock State

Costello, Gene—Slippery Rock
  (right)

Peterson, Ben—Iowa State (left)

Clinton, a 167–pound NCAA champion, works for near fall points in a duel with Oklahoma.

Clinton shown here breaking down Iowa State opponent at the 1962 NCAA Wrestling Championship.

Conrad, Roy—Northern Illinois University vs. Don Millard—Southern Illinois University (Carbondale)

Roy Conrad (NCAA Champion 1963) defends against single leg attack of NCAA Champion Don Millard (1960) in the finals of the first Midlands ever.

Clinton, Ronnie—Oklahoma State (top)

Kemp, Lee—Wisconsin

"Someone once said that Lee didn't wrestle like he was capable of wrestling. I replied maybe you're right, but by not wrestling like he's capable of it has taken him to three NCAA and two World Championship Golds."
    Stan Dziedzic
    United States National Coach

"The record books show him to be America's most accomplished collegiate and international wrestler."
    Duane Kleven
    Head Coach, University of Wisconsin

"His room is decorated in early half-nelson."
    Sports Illustrated

"I wouldn't say he's the best. There's people out there better than him. We just don't know their names."
Lee Kemp, Sr.

"One of America's most competitive and successful international wrestlers, primarily responsible for Wisconsin's unparalleled freestyle success."
Duane Kleven
Head Coach, University of Wisconsin

Hellickson, Russ—Wisconsin (front, in control)

Carollo, Nick—Adams State (right)

Carollo is about to reverse Tom Hazell from Oklahoma State in action at the 1972 Southern Open.

Christenson, Pat—Wisconsin (bottom)

"A talented performer who put it all together to win his 1976 NCAA title."
Duane Kleven
Head Coach, University of Wisconsin

McCann, Terry—Iowa University (foreground)

Hawkeye National and Olympic Champion demonstrates proper hand control and hip positioning during a standup attempt.

"Colgate's first Eastern Champion and quite a young man."
Curt Blake
Head Coach, Colgate University

Leslie, Steve—Colgate (top)

Henson, Joe—Navy (right)

Shrugs his Russian opponent by for a takedown during the finals of the 1952 Olympics.

Two of the country's best light heavyweights square off. Between them they were in the NCAA Finals five times!

McGlory, Cleo—University of Oklahoma (bottom)
Smith, Jason—Iowa State (top)

"The best ever out of the state of Wyoming. During his high school and college career he never lost a dual match."
   Dr. Everett Lantz
   Former University of Wyoming Head Coach

Not too often did anyone put this three-time NCAA Champion on his nose. Although Lindblad of Sweden scored on this move during the 1952 Olympics, he lost the match.

Hodge, Dan—University of Oklahoma (bottom)

All-American Pickard rides his Iowa foe with a nearside half in a close match.

Pickard, Tom—Iowa State (top)

108

Evans, Tommy—University of Oklahoma (standing)

In every bout, someone is destined to be the hammer and the other the anvil. Bard of Egypt is about to receive another blow from the American Sooner.

Peterson, John— Stout State

"The type of all-American that inspires
all who have had the pleasure to watch
him work out or compete."
Noel Loban
NCAA Champion

A National Champion as an athlete and
today a familiar figure in the Iowa
Winners Circle.

Robinson, Jay—Oklahoma State (lifting)

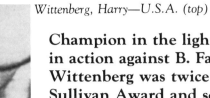

Champion in the light heavyweight division, in action against B. Fahlkvist of Sweden. Wittenberg was twice nominated for the Sullivan Award and scored 629 votes to finish in final balloting behind Mathias, Dillard, and Verdeur.

"He was the first wrestler I ever had the pleasure of watching that could pull a single leg to him using only one finger. Greg Gibson was the second."

Wade Schalles

Rohn, Don—Clarion State (lifting)

Rose to Spartan's challenge and grabbed title on 6-2 decision.

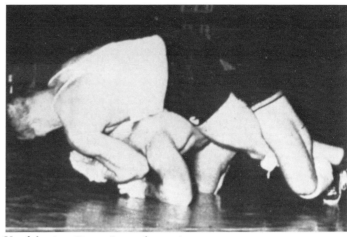

Kurdelmeier, Gary—Iowa (bottom)

Callard, Jeff—Oklahoma University (right)

113

Ward, Kelly—Iowa State (facing)

"Many ingredients make a good wrestler and Kelly had them all, but emotion was his forte."

Reinwand, Jack—Wisconsin (lifting)

"His accomplishments were exceeded only by his desire to accomplish more."
Duane Kleven,
Head Coach, University of Wisconsin

Houska, Harry—Ohio (control)

"Harry never showed emotion, whether winning, which he did a lot of, or
in defeat."
    Jim Howard
    Head Coach, Oswego State

Gotch, Frank—Legend

"The father of Amateur Wrestling in the state of Iowa and probably the
United States. Under the word "stud" in the dictionary, there can be
found a photo of this individual."

"His name is synonymous with strength and quality."
    Mike Chapman
    Cedar Rapids Gazette

FLOOD AND TORNADO SCENES

THE NATIONAL POLICE GAZETTE

THE LEADING ILLUSTRATED SPORTING JOURNAL IN THE WORLD.

COPYRIGHTED FOR 1913 BY RICHARD K. FOX PUBLISHING COMPANY, THE FOX BUILDING, FRANKLIN SQUARE, NEW YORK CITY

RICHARD K. FOX
President and Editor.

NEW YORK: SATURDAY, APRIL 19, 1913.

VOLUME CII. No. 1862
Price, 10 Cents.

CHAMPION FRANK GOTCH.
RETAINED HIS TITLE BY BEATING GEORGE LURICH AT KANSAS CITY HE IS THE
AUTHOR OF THE POLICE GAZETTE BOOK ON WRESTLING.

Schalles, Wade—Clarion State College

"Wonderous Wade Schalles, the most prolific master of the pin in
the history of NCAA wrestling."
   Norm Palovcsik
   Head Coach
   Penn State—Altoona Campus

Schalles, Wade—Clarion State College

Schalles, Wade—Clarion State College

Schalles, Wade—Clarion State College

"The most exciting wrestler to ever compete on a wrestling mat. If all performed like Wade—wrestling halls would always be filled."

Bert Kraus
United States Wrestling Champ

" Wonderous Wade—He was everything they said he was."

Bob Bubb
Head Coach, Clarion State

119

Johnson, Evan—Minnesota

"One of the most pleasant surprises I've ever coached."
  Wally Johnson
  Head Coach, University of Minnesota

Reiss, Matt—North Carolina State
(facing) (above) and (lifting) (right)

"He never stopped believing he could win a national title."

Bob Guzzo
Head Coach, North Carolina State

Cripps, Bill—Arizona State (top)

"A great competitor and a super human
 being."
    Bob Douglas
    Head Coach, Arizona State University

124

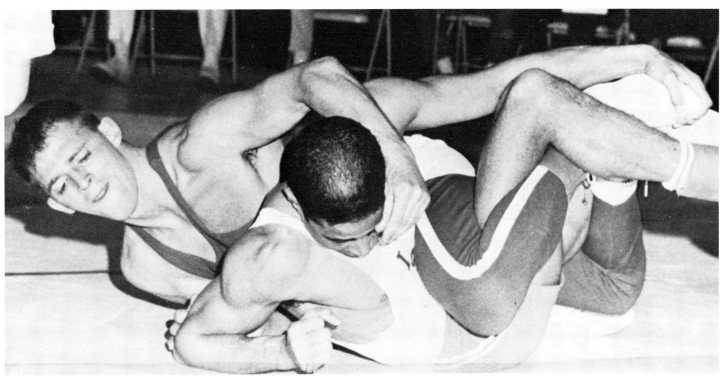

Drietzler, Jim—Moorhead State (in control)

"One of the first eastern wrestlers to defect to the midwest and make good. A winner in every respect."
Jim Howard
Head Coach, Oswego State

Sheppard, Israel—Oklahoma University (lifting)

Israel Sheppard shows cyclone Tom Pickard a quick way to the mat.

Boyd, Wayne—Temple (right)

"The only NCAA Champion in Temple wrestling history with an undefeated senior year and 33 wins."
Wrestling Office
Temple University

Mu came to America after an already successful career in Korea and continued it as a member of the Athletes in Action–East.

Chang, Mu—Athletes in Action (bottom)

Gross, Steve—University of Tennessee-Chattanooga (throwing)

"Steve Gross' execution of technique was so beautiful that it could have been put to music."
   Jim Morgan
   Head Coach, University of Tennessee-Chattanooga

McCann, Terry—United States Gold Medalist (top) works on Poland's Trojanowski.

"Terry was fast and tough. He was a lightweight with the strength of a heavyweight."
Joe Scalzo
Amateur Athletics Union

Young, Keith—Iowa Teachers

Young defeated Jim Maurey in this NCAA semi-final match at Cedar Falls and went on to win the 145-pound title.

Breece, Gary—Oklahoma University (top)
NCAA Champion 1974

One of the most successful Sooners to ever wear the crimson and cream.

Johnson, Johnny—Penn State

"A classic example of no pain-no gain. Johnny reached the NCAA Division 1 Championships with severe arthritis in his ankles."
Don Flavin
Head Coach, Northern Illinois University

Obviously, a full head of hair and youth are not prerequisites for success in wrestling.

Russia vs. Sweden—1952 Olympics Finals

"One of the most physical wrestlers I have seen."
Frank McCann
Head Coach, Indiana State University

Tedder of Oklahoma A&M spills Gene Franklin as Cowpokes defeat Georgia Tech in Atlanta (1948).

DeWitt, Ed

Winner over the Italian Caraffini.

Duane Keller is determined to get a "tilt" during United States Wrestling Federation freestyle.

Keller, Duane—Oklahoma State (controlling)

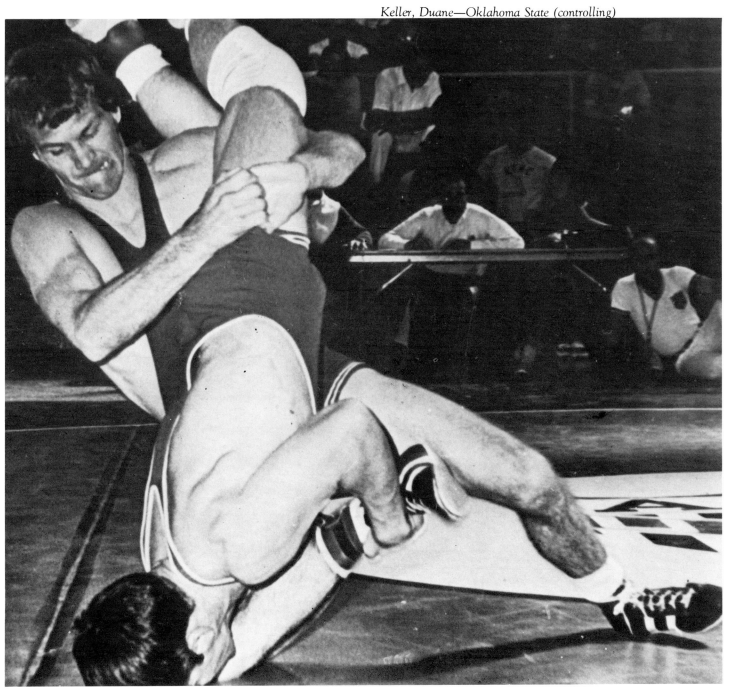

"A gifted wrestler who could turn anybody with a bar-arm and half. He revived the modern day crab ride.
   Tom was lost to the wrestling world by way of a traffic accident in 1979."
      Bob Bubb
      Head Coach, Clarion State

Terrapin 123-pounder and present Head Coach, John McHugh, controls North Carolina State opponent in 1955 dual meet at College Park, Maryland.

McHugh, John—Maryland (top)

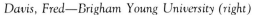
Davis, Fred—Brigham Young University (right)

Davis seems stalemated at this point, but went on to win the match and the title at the 1955 NCAA Championships.

Hodge, Dan—Oklahoma University (shown pinning another opponent)

"If the criterion for the greatest wrestler is the highest percentage of falls, then Dan's record is tough to equal."
Don Sayenga
Amateur Wrestling News Historian

Hodge posted an overall record of 38-0 with 36 of those wins coming by fall.

The only coach in the East to ever
win the NCAA team title.

Speidel, Charlie—Penn State University (1927-64)

Beatson, Brian—Oklahoma (top)

**Talented Brian Beatson tries to control Mike
Frick in their NCAA Final at 134 pounds.
Frick won the championship and the OW
Award for the 1975 season.**

Phinney, Dean—Iowa (bottom)

"When the opportunity came for Dean to
perform, he did so in fine fashion."
Dan Gable
Head Coach, University of Iowa

Keller, Darrell—Oklahoma State University (bottom)

Vs NCAA Champion Barry Owens in 1971 finals—Keller won a thriller 16-12.

Dellagatta, Ricky—Kentucky (in control)

"A real crowd-pleaser; extremely persistent and dedicated."
Fletcher Carr
Head Coach, University of Kentucky

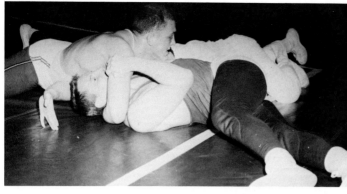

Sandusky, Mike—Maryland (top)

His four collegiate wrestling seasons provided the base for his years as all-pro in the National Football League.

Callahan, Curt—Maryland (in control)

Wrestling made him the footballer he is today.

Culp, Curley—Arizona State (right)

141

"The first NCAA place-winner ever from Shippensburg State and a rider extraordinaire."
Anonymous

Burket, Glenn—Shippensburg (top)

"A fiery competitor."
Fred Davis
Coach—Brigham Young University

McAdams, Russ—Brigham Young University

Oishi, Hachiro—New York Athletic Club (bottom)

**"One of the great throwers. Shown here competing
in the sombo nationals."**
   Sonny Greenhalgh
   Head Coach, New York Athletic Club

McCready, Mike—University of Northern Iowa

"Smart and dedicated. Intensity and attitude carried him to National titles in wrestling and track."
Chuck Patton
Head Coach, University of Northern Iowa

This bout decided who was the American representative in the 1960 Olympic Games. Shelby won the bout and the Gold.

Engineer Jim Reilly of Lehigh rides cyclone Perry Hummel of Iowa State during a home duel in Bethlehem.

Morgan, Larry—Cal Poly (left)

**Larry Morgan is trying to counter Butch
Keaser's bear hug as official Bob Pankake
monitors the action.**

146

Douglas, Bobby—Oklahoma State (in control)

"One of the greatest wrestlers in the world."
Gene Davis
Olympian

Hanson, Brad—Brigham Young University (foreground)

Cyclone Dave Powell successfully countered this takedown attempt but lost the bout to Hanson of Brigham Young University.

In front of 8,300 fans, Bob Wilson delivers his Oklahoma opponent Lawrence Gregory to the mat . . .

Wilson, Bob—Oklahoma State (top) (1961)

McGuire, David—Oklahoma (left)

Referee Bob Siddens keeps a close watch on Dave McGuire and Mike Riley of Oklahoma State in 1969 NCAA action.

Owings, Larry—University of Washington (top)

"Larry was a very unique competitor. His style allowed him to jump from one weight class to another and realize tremendous success."

Keith Young
Olympian.

The Bedlam series continues as Harlow squares off against Oklahoma's Luke Sharp.

Harlow, Bill—Oklahoma State (facing)

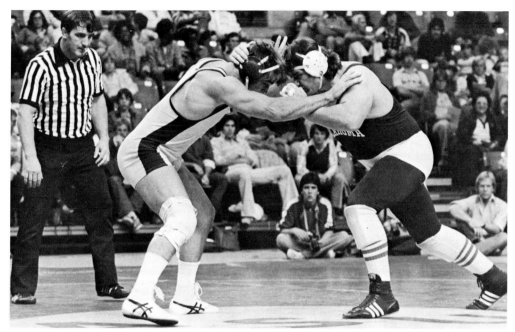

Williams, Steve—Oklahoma University (right)

"The imposing stature and wrestling style of this Sooner led to the media's nicknaming him Dr. Death."
    Norm Palovcsik
    Head Coach,
    Penn State-Altoona Campus

With only nine years of coaching, Ed earned the title "Dean of coaches" with eight national titles.

A hell of a double.

"Jim was as quick as a cat and a big one at that."
Ed Carlen
Head Coach, Syracuse University

Nance, Jim—Syracuse (standing)

Being declared an early round winner over Johannsson of Sweden in the 1952 Olympics.

Garrell, Shawn—Oklahoma University

Garell is trying to find a way to turn Tom Brown of Michigan in the 1975 NCAA finals.

Jack Ellena—of University of California Los Angeles (Bruins) **is about to pin Al Mosten of California (Bears) in Pacific Coast Conference match. Ellena won Coast's heavyweight crown, as well as this dual meet bout.**

"An exceptionally quick-learning young athlete who put that God-given skill to use in a positive way."
Ken Kraft
Associate Athletic Director, Northwestern University

Allen, Andre—Northwestern

Art Baker controls Tim Woodin of Michigan State in their NCAA championship final. Baker emerged the winner 9-5.

Baker, Art—Syracuse NCAA Champ

"One of the great links in a long chain of Dale Thomas heavyweights.

Bielenberg, Larry—Oregon State University (top)

DeStefanis, Carl—Penn State University

Level change, penetration and intensity are must ingredients for success on one's feet.

"Exceptional mat wrestler. Self motivated,
hard worker, and very dedicated."
Ed Perry
Head Coach, United States Naval Academy

Reich, John—Navy (top)

"A tremendous coach, athlete, and recruiter. Probably one of the last strict disciplinarians."
Bob Fehrs
Head Coach, University of Nebraska

You can neutralize one's ability to bridge by isolating the chin and turning the head as shown by another one of the many NCAA Champions from Iowa State.

Quintana, Rod—George Mason University (hidden)

"He had no takedowns so
he learned a spladle."
Mike Connor
Head Coach, George Mason University

Brown, Jim—Michigan University

"Dynamite in a small package"—Jim's "never quit" attitude and constant motion fired up four Michigan teams to NCAA prominence...
Michigan Athletic Department

Tony Gizoni—of Waynesburg.

He not only overcame his opponent here, Frank Altman of Iowa Teachers, but he went on to win the NCAA 121-pound competition so impressively that he was selected as the tourney's outstanding entrant.

Ohai, Ben—Brigham Young University (bottom)

"One of the best ever. Ben was a great takedown technician."
Fred Davis
Coach, Brigham Young University

"Randy was one of the most gifted and exciting wrestlers I have ever coached, a national wrestling phenomenon."
Jim Morgan
Head Coach,
University of Tennesee-Chattanooga

McGlory, Cleo—Oklahoma (left)

Two points for the takedown are awarded to Cleo McGlory in this match with Jim Guyer of Northern Iowa.

The year was 1973, the place was Seattle—Dan Sherman counters a single leg attack by Glass of Iowa State. Sherman won the bout and the NCAA title.

Sherman, Dan—Iowa

Murdock, Bill—Washington (top)

Washington's Bill Murdock goes for a nearside cradle against Minnesota's John Panning in the 1972 Nationals.

"A great and unorthodox wrestler who developed his style into an NCAA championship."
Ed Perry
Head Coach, United States Naval Academy

Muthler, Dan—Navy

Koll, Bill—North Iowa (Iowa State Teachers)

"The meanest, toughest, and most aggressive takedown wrestler in collegiate circles."
Head Coach
Penn State 1965-78

"Mike was without a doubt one of the best upperweight wrestlers in the down position. He could roll."
Anonymous

Brown, Mike—Lehigh (defending single leg)

Holm, Dan—Iowa (in control)

"He seemed to enjoy punishing his opponents as much as defeating them—just downright mean."
Dan Gable
Head Coach, University of Iowa

Steve is the glue that holds a family of winners together.

Woods, Jim—Western Illinois (top)

"NCAA champion, a big accomplishment for a big man."
Joe Protsman
Head Coach, Western Illinois University

**Attacks the legs of Hawkeye Bruce Kinseth
and came away with a 6-0 victory.**

Zuspann, Joe—Iowa State (left)

Zilverberg, Larry—Minnesota (top)

The setting is the 1974 NCAA Finals at 158 pounds . . . The Golden
Gopher controlled this period but lost the bout and the title to Rod
Kilgore of Oklahoma.

"A fine lad of German descent who had a knack for winning."
Dale Thomas
Head Coach, Oregon State University

Knorr, Dick—Oregon State (doing a firemens)

Banach, Lou—Iowa (right)

"A very talented person who can be a big help in one's total effort for success."
Dan Gable
Head Coach, University of Iowa

Mr. Excitement.

"Like most of our best United States wrestlers, Gene never loses but occasionally runs out of time when the score is not in his favor."

Stan Dziedzic
US National Coach

"Simply stated, mean Gene the pinning machine."
Ed Carlen
Head Coach, Syracuse University

177

Mock, C. D.—University of North Carolina (top)

Another hard-nosed Bill Lam product.

"A consistent winner and leader in four varsity campaigns."
Duane Kleven
Head Coach, University of Wisconsin

Evans, Dave—Wisconsin

178

"The fastest wrestler I've ever coached."
Harold Nichols
Head Coach, Iowa State

Carr, Nate—Iowa State (right)

Nelson, Kenny—Oklahoma University (bottom)

Nelson is on the attack, but about to be countered by Nick Gallo of Hofstra.

To the aggressor go the spoils!

Kenny Monday, Oklahoma (facing) vs. Wade Potter, Lock Haven State (troubled)

The legacy of Billy Martin Sr. rolls on.

Chris Catalfo, Syracuse (top) vs. Johnny Johnson, Oklahoma (bottom)

Adam Cuestas, California State-Bakersfield (standing)
vs. Al Palacio, North Carolina (praying)

"I hope this Resilite is as resilient as they advertise!"

Wrestling is still more than just being proficient on your feet. For disbelievers, the doctor prescribes three minutes under John Reich.

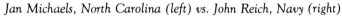

Jan Michaels, North Carolina (left) vs. John Reich, Navy (right)

A bright young man from Princeton has just made a fatal mistake in the NCAA finals; the bout ended by fall moments later.

Jackson, Jimmy — Oklahoma State University (top)

All-American Rod Kilgore dances away from Mark Lieberman of Lehigh during the NCAA Finals.

Kilgore, Rod—Oklahoma University (right)

"By far one of the finest big men I have ever had the pleasure to coach. Has the potential to be one of the best heavyweights in the world."
Fran McCann
Head Coach, Indiana State University

Baumgartner, Bruce—Indiana State (top)

"Quite tall in stature and character."
Dale Thomas
Head Coach,
Oregon State University

Harold Smith vs. Howard Harris — Oregon State

"Always seemed to be ready when it really counted, during the NCAAs."
Dan Gable
Head Coach, University of Iowa

Trizzino, Scott — University of Iowa

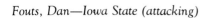
Fouts, Dan—Iowa State (attacking)

The cardinal and gold of Iowa State goes for a single leg against three-time National Champion— Jimmy Jackson.

Shelton, Charles—Oklahoma University (top)

Shelton begins to smell victory—his opponent, the mat.

Zilverberg, Dan—Minnesota

"He and his brother Larry were two of the most dedicated and hard-working wrestlers that I have had."
Wally Johnson
Head Coach, University of Minnesota

Spinning out of a Russion two-on-one was good for the takedown against Cowboy Jerry Kelly.

Gasner, Marvin — University of Colorado (foreground)

A firemens with a twist...a Wais
trademark in 1979 when he won the
NCAA title at 190 lbs.

McAuther, Mike—Minnesota

"Excellent competitor—full of confidence."
Wally Johnson
Head Coach, University of Minnesota

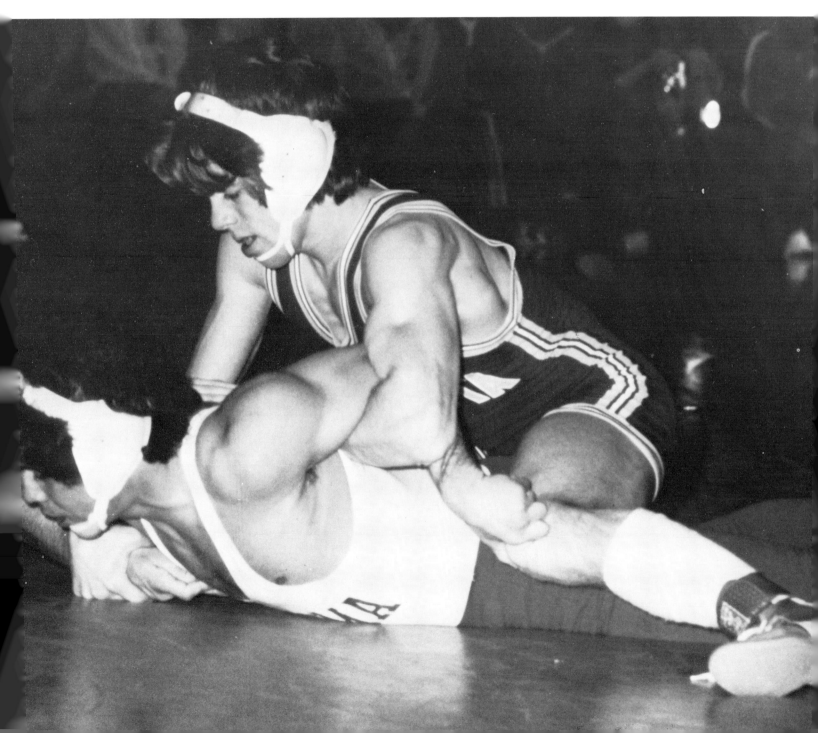

Harlan Kistler, Iowa (right) vs. Al Freeman, Nebraska (left)

Takedowns don't necessarily have to be pretty. It's second effort that gets results!

"Jim possessed what might have been the best single-leg attack in the history of the sport."
   Duane Kleven
   Head Coach, University of Wisconsin

Haines, Jim — Wisconsin (bottom)

"A coach's dream. He fits the mold of a champion—always dangerous and exceptionally strong."
    Bobby Douglas
    Head Coach,
    Arizona State University

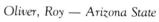

Oliver, Roy — Arizona State

Phillips, Tom—Oregon State University (left)

"Quite short but his opponents didn't think so small."
    Dale Thomas
    Head Coach, Oregon State University

Cook, Gary—East Stroudsburg State (in control)
Bradley, Mike

"During his era, there were not too many men who were more intense or meaner!"
    Jim Howard
    Head Coach, Oswego State

"Quick and tough—he beat many of the best!"
    Red Whitman
    Athletic Director,
    East Stroudsburg State

"Mr. Cool—always steady."
    Grady Peninger
    Head Coach, Michigan State

"One of the strongest and best conditioned athletes we've ever had."
    Duane Kleven
    Head Coach, University of Wisconsin

"A tremendous competitor with a great desire to be the best."
    Ron Finley
    Head Coach, University of Oregon

Jeidy, Ron — Wisconsin

Bliss, Scott — Oregon (left)

193

Hicks, Dan—Oregon State (right)

All-American and National Champion Dan Hicks is about to switch Iowa's Scott Trizzino in NCAA action.

Harris, Howard — Oregon State (top)

**"Quite tall in stature and character."
Dale Thomas
Head Coach, Oregon State University**

"One of the greatest young wrestlers America ever produced."
    Gene Davis
    Olympian

Shultz, Dave — Oklahoma University (bottom)

Germundson flurries with an Oklahoma Sooner in a typical OSU—OU showdown.

Germundson, Gary—Oklahoma State University (top)

Stearns, Keith—Oklahoma University

Keith Bridges backs into his opponent hoping to gain a defensive pin.

"One of the strongest athletes I've ever been around. He lifted Jimmy Jackson over his head during their bout."
Fletcher Carr
Head Coach, University of Kentucky

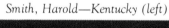

Smith, Harold—Kentucky (left)

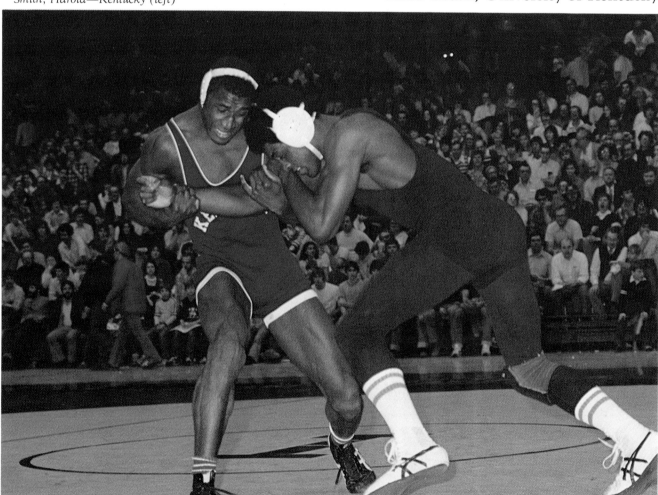

The cyclone grappler goes for back points against his nemesis from Iowa, Randy Lewis.

Land, Mike—Iowa State (top)

Lee Roy has Colorado's Lou
Sondgeroth off balance with a picture
book duck-under.

Smith, Lee Roy — Oklahoma State University (facing)

Puebla, Kevin — Illinois (left)

"A great natural athlete whose
cat-like quickness made him
formidable on his feet."
        Greg Johnson
        Head Coach,
        University of Illinois

198

Another Oklahoma/Oklahoma State shootout . . . as Paul Martin tries desperately to shake the ride of Keith Stearns in the NCAA Finals.

Martin, Paul—Oklahoma State (bottom)

Wais and Mark Lieberman battle it out in NCAA action

Wais, Eric — Oklahoma State (left, bottom)

199

DeAngelis, Frank—Oklahoma (red)

DeAngelis tries to elude the ride of Oklahoma State's Lee Roy Smith.

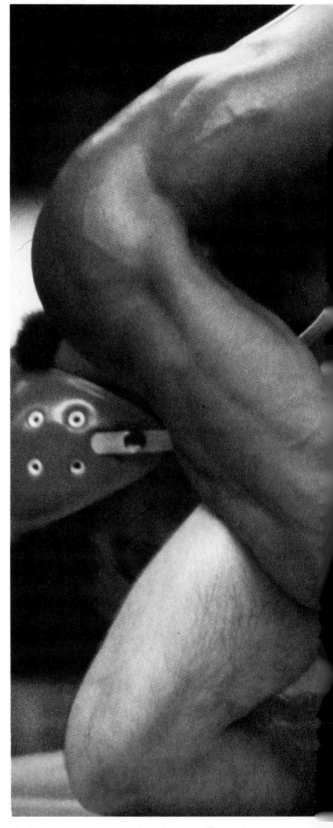

Becker, Dave — Pennsylvania State (bottom)

"Dave was extremely strong and one of the best takedown men in the country. He had but one real problem—Lee Kemp (top)."
Rich Lorenzo
Head Coach, Pennsylvania State

Stewart, Ricky — Oklahoma State (right)

"As exciting to watch as anyone I've ever seen wrestle. A real pleasure to have been his coach."
   Dan Gable
   Head Coach, University of Iowa

Lewis, Randy—Iowa (bottom)

Jackson, Jimmy — Oklahoma State University (top)

A bright young man from Princeton has just made a fatal mistake in the NCAA finals; the bout ended by fall moments later.

Allen, Dave — Iowa State (bottom)

"To have come so far and to find a roadblock named — Banach."

Rein, Andy—Wisconsin

"Mike's strength, I believe, was his
determination and his want to excel."
Jim Harold
FILA

"A great person who seems to do things
more for others than himself. Definitely
one of my 'favorites' in terms of enjoying
to coach and to just be around."
Dan Gable
Head Coach, University of Iowa

Daniels, Andy — Ohio University (lifting)

Didn't he wrestle 134?

**"The biggest 118-pounder that America
has ever produced."
John Hartupee
Central Michigan University**

Kinseth (bottom right)

Burley, Darryl—Lehigh University (right)

A four time all-American who couldn't be shaken mentally.

Radman, George—Michigan State (right)

"Great physical strength with technique."
Grady Peninger
Head Coach, Michigan State

Rein, Andy—Wisconsin

"His upper body attack and physical intensity could
make him one of the best Badgers ever."
Duane Kleven
Head Coach, University of Wisconsin

Kristoff, Larry—Southern Illinois University

"A great heavyweight who if he had
a weakness it would be countering
the Russian two on one."
Richard Volvia
Olympian

NAAU 1967, Larry Kristoff vs. Curley Culp

Larry Kristoff — 1966 World Championship Heavyweight

Brouhard, Dave—San Jose State (lifting)

"Although not a very successful high school athlete, it was a pleasure to see David achieve NCAA all–American honors."
Terry Kerr
Head Coach, San Jose State

Detwiller going for the fall against foe from Lock Haven State.

Detwiller, Al—East Stroudburg State (hidden & in control)

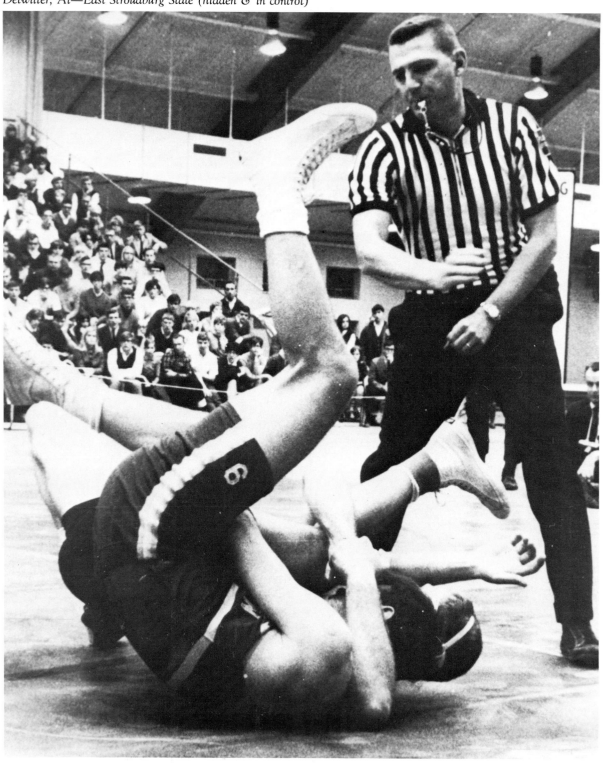

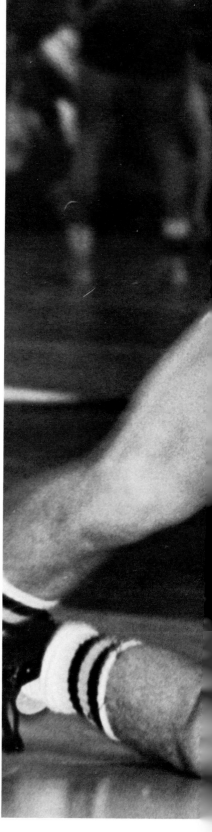

"A great all-American."
Bob Guzzo
Head Coach, North Carolina State

His Franklin & Marshall opponent will go no
further than this attempted standup against this
all-Ivy and all-American heavyweight from
Princeton.

Sefter, John—Princeton (top)

Wells, Wayne—Oklahoma (top)

Headed for the gold . . . Wayne Wells rides Seger of West Germany in the finals of the 72 Munich Olympics.

Stanley, Herbert—Adams State College (top)

Herbert Stanley, a 2-time NAIA heavyweight champion from Adams State College, overpowers his opponent from Colorado University.

Reeve, Ethan—Tennessee (lifting)

"Ethan was the master of the single leg series."
    Gray Simons
    Head Coach, Tennessee

Pendleton, Kirk—Lehigh (top)

Pendleton rides Army Cadet Tom Thompson to an 8-0 victory in 1963 dual meet.

Black, Chris—Franklin & Marshall (top)

One of the best 126-pounders in the country in the early 1970's. Unfortunately, a series of events prevented Chris from proving that on the mat he was the best.

"He was obsessed by the notion he could pin anyone; usually he did so with ease. No one ever defeated him."
Don Sayenga
Amateur Wrestling News Historian

Vaughan's son, Steve, forces Ratchford of the Air Force Academy to the mat while cruising to a 5-0 victory.

Hitchcock, Steve—Cal Poly (control)

Mozier, Frank —Moorhead State

"The most flexible and diversified wrestler I've ever
coached."
Bill Garland
Head Coach, Morehead State

"He couldn't wait for you to take him down so he could pin you. He knew what pinning was all about and many a wrestler felt his pin pressure."

Jim Howard
Head Coach, Oswego State

Eichelberger, Eddie—Lehigh (top)

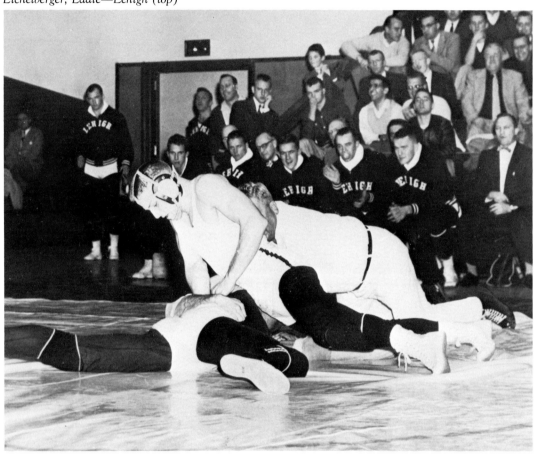

Martin, Dave—Iowa State (right)

Ray, Ron—Oklahoma State (right)

Consistency was what carried Ron to an NCAA title, that and a firemen's that wasn't all that shabby.

1969 NCAA tournament action finds Dave Martin countering the attack of Oklahoma's Cleo McClory.

Hesson, Stan—Oklahoma State (right)

"Art Griffith and Edward Gallagher cited
Henson as the best man they'd ever coached."
Don Sayenga
Amateur Wrestling News

Rains, Grover—Oklahoma A&M

A single leg attack is being utilized to defeat
Penn State's Mike Rubino during their 1951
NCAA bout where Rains won the match
and the title.
Life Magazine

Watts, Randy—Bloomsburg (right) vs Pete Galea, Iowa State

"Hard work and determination best describes Randy Watts. He has a heart the size of a wrestling mat."
Roger Sanders
Head Coach, Bloomsburg State, Pennsylvania

"A true artist with the high crotch."

Hatta, Masaaki—Oklahoma State University (turning opponent)

Jack Moreno—Purdue

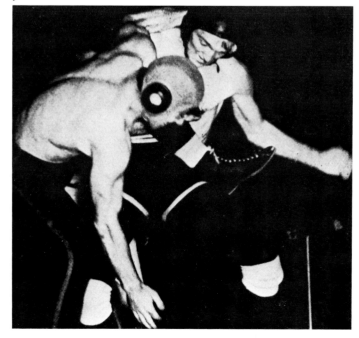

Jack Moreno of Purdue and Keith Young of Iowa Teachers are caught in a mid-air pose in their final bout in the NCAA 145-pound division. Young went on to win the bout and title, but not without a good struggle by the Big Ten champ Moreno.

Lieberman, Mark—Lehigh

"He may not be the most talented wrestler in the country, but he's the gutsiest—and the best."
Sports Illustrated

**Over the years, the American-Russian matches have been
intensely competitive.**

Spates, Jack—Slippery Rock State (facing)

"Amicable, a fine technician and a winner."
Fred Powell
Head Coach, Slippery Rock State

"The man no one thought could win the big one. For, you see, he
never won even a sectional tournament while in high school, and yet
won an NCAA Division 1 National Championship."
Bob Bubb
Head Coach, Clarion State

Hitchcock, Floyd—Bloomsburg State (botto

"One of the most physical wrestlers ever
step on a wrestling mat, his desire to wi
being his strongest attribute
Roger Sande
Head Coach, Bloomsburg State, Pennsylvan

Another thoroughbred trained and groomed by Bobby Douglas.

**"His ability as a wrestler was surpassed only
by his love of the sport."
Fred Davis
Coach, Brigham Young University**

"Pound for pound the quickest and most explosive wrestler of the century."
Jim Howard
Head Coach, Oswego State

"One of the most physical middleweights that ever stepped on the mat. He had this thing for gold."

"Damn if it wasn't nice watching him pancake Habbi of Iran for the second time to secure a pin and win the gold in the Rome Olympics."
Joe Scalzo
Amateur Athletics Union

Simons, Gray—U.S.A.
(Lock Haven State)

Knocking down his antagonist, the Mexican Rosato.

Simons, Gray—Lock Haven State (control)

"Besides his tremendous wrestling ability, Grey was always Mr.
Congeniality. I always wanted my sons to grow up and be the same
quality of human being."
    Jim Howard
    Head Coach, Oswego State

"He could duck under a groundhog and ankle-pick an elephant to
his back in his prime."

Gadson, Willie—Iowa State (left)

A competitor in the Iowa State mold, strong and durable.

"Our first NCAA Champion: Rick was too mentally tough to lose."
Duane Kleven
Head Coach, University of Wisconsin

Lawinger, Rich—Wisconsin (left)

Behm, Don—Michigan State University (top)

"An exciting wrestler and an exceptional technician on his feet."
Bert Kraus
National Wrestling Official

"Unbeatable on offense!"
Grady Peninger
Head Coach, Michigan State

"Probably the finest technician I've ever had the pleasure to watch in competition."
   Bob Fehrs
   Head Coach, University of Nebraska

"The finest collegiate wrestler that ever lived."
   Joe Scalzo
   FILA Representative

"The greatest wrestler in the world during his time."
   Gene Davis
   Olympian

Sofman, Rich—NYCA (top)

Smelling the sweet aroma of victory, Rich Sofman works for the fall.

Howard, Jim—Ithaca College (right, in control)

"A wrestler who paid the price and reaped the benefits."
    Richard Volvia
    Olympian

Greatest legs in wrestling.

"An example that real desire and willingness to work pays off."
Red Whitman
Athletic Director, East Stroudsburg State

Rossi, Dan—East Stroudsburg State (left)

Greenhalgh, Sonny—New York Athletic Club (top)

"A very consistent performer."

Without his guidance and dedication, the New York Athletic Club might not have achieved national prominence and maintained it for so long.

"Possesses a great deal of determination and strength."
Bobby Douglas
Head Coach, Arizona State

Severn, Dan—Arizona State University (bottom)

Powell, Fred—Lock Haven (left)

NCAA champion Fred Powell refuses to let his opponent get away in 1966 world championships.

Stanley, Jerry—Oklahoma University (bottom)

"One of the greatest coaches that I've known who never had a desire to be a head coach. Probably the Number 1 assistant coach in the country..."
Jim Howard
Head Coach, Oswego State

Zuaro, Vince—New York (far right)

248

"Vince has done more to promote international officiating than any
other American."
Burt Kraus
United States Wrestling Official

Caruso, Mike—Lehigh University (left)

"Mr. Duckunder", the most successful athlete in Lehigh history.

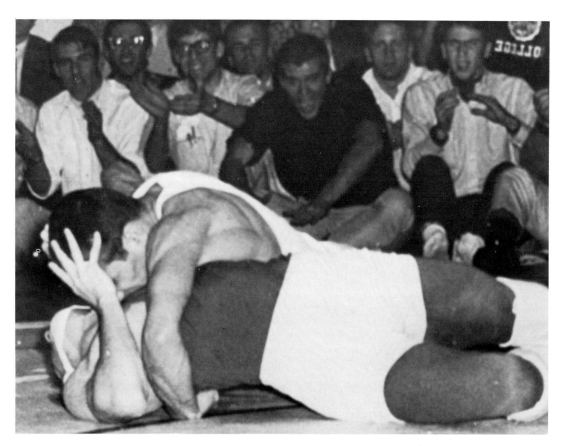

Caruso, Mike—Lehigh University (top)

250

DePaoli, Bill—California State, Pennsylvania (top)

"One of the best California State has ever produced and quite a man he is."

Frank Volcano
Head Coach, California State, Pennsylvania

Lehman, Gerald—Iowa Teachers College (top)

Bushong, Ned (in control) vs. Bob Larson.

"A tremendous competitor and the father of Lehigh Wrestling."
  Richard Volvia
  Olympian

"Followed the legend of Billy Sheridan as a coach at Lehigh and surpassed the master in dedication to the sport of wrestling."
  Jim Howard
  Head Coach, Oswego State

"One of the best mat wrestling coaches around."

"A tremendous coach and wrestler. Mentally tough."
  Richard Volvia
  Olympian

Sculley, Tom—Lehigh (left)

Lehigh got its first National Champion of the 1974 Nationals in Tom Sculley as he counters Jimmy Miller's double leg attempt.

"Nature did not award him with quickness, a most important quality
  for the good wrestler. Ned adapted, had his own style and proved to be
  a consistent winner and pinner."
  Red Whitman
  Athletic Director, East Stroudsburg State

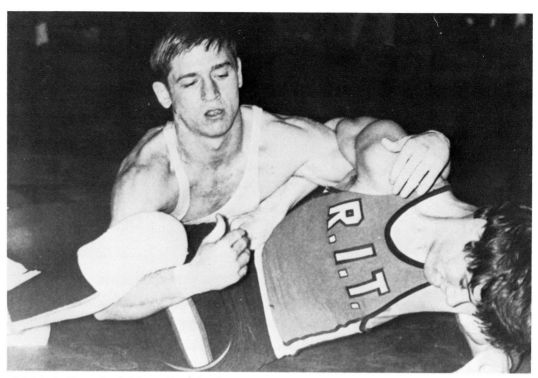

Melchoir, Ken—Lock Haven State (top)

...was one of only a small handful of National Champions that could be classified as a "great leg wrestler."

Cvestas, Dan—Cal State, Bakersfield (top)

Dave Cooke of North Carolina lost his takedown and the title by the score of 7-5 during the 1981 NCAA Championships.

Connor, Mike—Emerson College (left)

"One of the most capable officials both internationally and collegiately."
Fernando Compte
Vice-President, F.I.L.A.

Morrison, Tim — Rider (top)

"Tim has time and again shown signs of greatness. Unfortunately the big one eluded him."
 Gary Taylor
 Head Coach, Rider College

Morrison, Dan—Rider (top)

"Dan has one of if not the greatest cradle series in collegiate wrestling history. His mental toughness enabled him to defeat 3 all-Americans during his career."
Gary Taylor
Head Coach, Rider College

Campbell, Jack — Clarion State (left)

"An all-American whose headlock will long be remembered by
Clarion fans and quite a few opponents."
Bob Bubb
Head Coach, Clarion State

258

Campbell, Chris — Iowa (attacking)

"His ability has been unequalled, and because of this his execution of techniques has been as close to perfect as I've seen."
     Dan Gable
     Head Coach, University of Iowa

Fritz, Bernie — Pennsylvania State

"Bernie was talented, explosive, and a
 takedown master. He was extremely
 pleasurable to watch."
  Rich Lorenzo
  Head Coach,
  Pennsylvania State

"A dynamic and explosive wrestler who did
not know the meaning of the word 'can't.'
There never was a mountain that was too
high for him."
Rich Lorenzo
Head Coach, Pennsylvania State

Fritz, John — Pennsylvania State

Fehlberg, Rondo — Brigham Young University

"His intensity as an athlete lasted four years and won him many matches."
    Fred Davis
    Coach, Brigham Young University

"Rondo and his brother Reed were two of four brothers that won 8
state high school titles for me at Worland, Wyoming. There was
one girl in the family—wish she was a boy!"

Lanny Bryant
Editor, Wrestling USA

Fehlberg, Reed — Brigham Young University

"He could rock any wrestler to sleep in his cradles, and did."
Fred Davis,
Coach, Brigham Young University

Milkovich, Tom — Michigan State University (right)

A great wrestler, great coach, and a great man.

"He and his brother Tom are two combinations of fierce pride."
Grady Peninger
Head Coach, Michigan State University

Milkovich, Pat — Michigan State University (bottom)

No wrestling room is complete without its pile of wet gear.

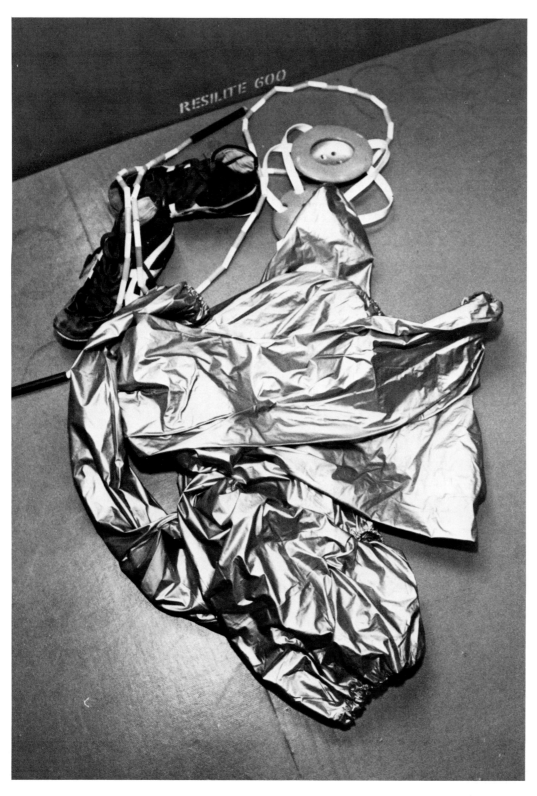

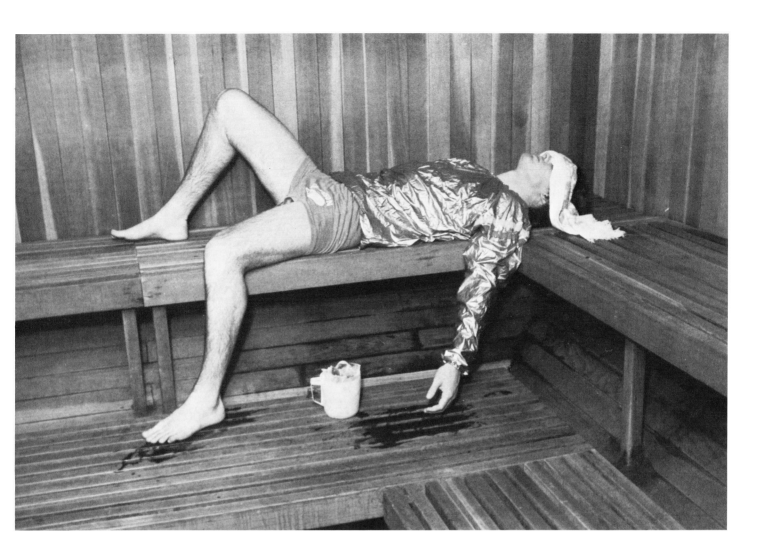

How could we have ever managed without a
hot box to control our fatness!

Metzger, Andre — Oklahoma University (bottom)

Mister Versatile, a legend in high school, Collegiate National Champion, and World Medalist.

Dick Knorr of Oregon State lifts Larry Kihlstadius of Navy
skyward during their NCAA semi-final bouts in 1979.

Knorr, Dick — Oregon State

Tell him the bowl for two
T-shirts and a pair of jeans.

Anybody ever complain about your socks before?

**Couldn't you just give it to me,
no one will know!**

Jim Gibbons—Iowa State (right) vs Jeff Kerber—Iowa (left)

The wrestlers of Iowa give the fans of Iowa wrestling and officiating at its best.

Lee, Buddy (Old Dominion University)-all-American

"His quickness was like nothing I've ever
  seen before."
    Pete Robinson
    Head Coach, Old Dominion University

Taylor, Jody—Clemson

"There were few slicker and none I cared for more."
Wade Schalles
Clemson University

Vance, Larry—Clemson

His infectious work ethic made him great.

**The author works for another fall in Tbilisi, Russia. Capitalism is
safe for at least one more round.**

Dotson won the 1963 NCAA Tournament by defeating Iowa's Tom Huff in the finals.

The 1950 NCAA Wrestling Championships reach the semi-final round.

Chris Taylor—Iowa State (facing) vs Jim Waschek—Iowa (concerned)

Chris won two NCAA titles and an Olympic Bronze before his untimely passing.

Siddens, Bob—Waterloo, Iowa (official)

Lewis, Randy—Iowa (top)

**The Hawkeye Olympian demonstrates the "back-to-basics" style that
became his trademark.**

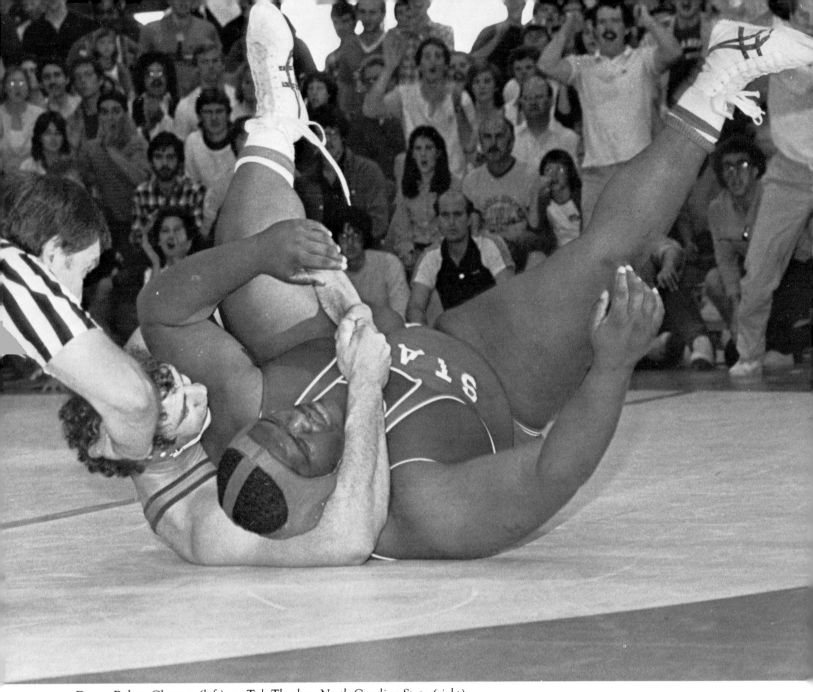

Duane Baker, Clemson (left) vs. Tab Thacker, North Carolina State (right)

To borrow a phrase, Duane "could rock anyone to
sleep, and often did!"

Simons, Gray—3-time NCAA Champion, 4-time NAIA Champion

Gray Simons (Lock Haven State) very seldom had to work for a takedown. This was an exception!

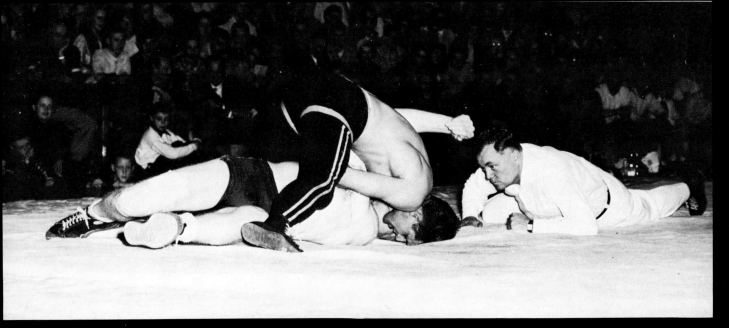

Koll, Bill—Iowa State Teachers (top)

He completed his collegiate career with a 72-0 record, three NCAA titles, and two Outstanding Wrestler awards.

Fujita, Yoshiro—Oklahoma State (in control)

Davis, Barry—Iowa

". . . tenacious, aggressive, and relentless!"
Steve Bernhardt
FILA Official

Hodge, Dan—Oklahoma (top, where else!)

This opponent was quoted as saying "For the first two periods I thought I was going to die. In the third I feared that I wouldn't."

Talons won this Hawk-Duck encounter during the 1982 NCAA Tournament.

*Lennie Zalesky (facing) vs
Bill Nugent—Oregon*